365

Thoughts of Peace & Harmony

WHITE STAR PUBLISHERS

365

Thoughts of Peace & Harmony

CONTENTS

MINDFULNESS, THE ART

Mindfulness, a practice that is only now gaining popularity in the West (so much so that we now talk unequivocally of a mindful revolution), makes it possible to truly be present in the "here and now." The idea is to bring one's attention to—and appreciate—every instant of life, making friends with the incessant changes that define it, embracing the flow of existence, in harmony with nature and others. In addition to reducing stress and anxiety and improving mood, mindfulness (which means "conscious attention") promotes psychological well-being and a calm, satisfied state of mind in the present moment, harmonizing with it and, ultimately, with one's life.

Thanks to modern-day adaptations of centuries-old meditative practices (with particular reference to Buddhist traditions) and their integration with recent developments in psychoeducation, programs based on mindfulness have gained widespread popularity around the world in the past few decades. Taking root in a variety of settings and segments of society, that development has been a response to the stress and mental fatigue caused by the frenetic rhythms and countless demands of everyday life as we know it.

At first, mindfulness was exclusively understood as a type of meditative path. Not surprisingly, the Dalai Lama has played an important role in the promotion of mindfulness as a practice in the West, thanks in large part to the Mind &

OF CONSCIOUS LIVING

Life Institute, which he founded with Francisco Varela, a philosopher, neuroscientist, and practicing Tibetan Buddhist. Others, like Matthieu Ricard (a Tibetan monk who has been called "the happiest person in the world" based on the findings of a study on his meditation capacities) and Daniel Goleman (a best-selling author who has collaborated with the Dalai Lama to write successful books on negative and positive emotions), have helped popularize meditative and contemplative practices. The same can be said of Vietnamese Zen master Thích Nhất Hạnh, who broadened the field of action, highlighting the benefits of meditation and mindfulness not just for the self, but also for the world around us. Fundamentally, human beings are part of an ecosystem, which can be positively influenced even when everything seems adversarial.

However, what has truly made mindfulness so successful and popular today is its potential as a method to improve people's lives, a way to treat psychological distress and even illness. Jon Kabat-Zinn, a biologist and professor emeritus at the University of Massachusetts Medical School, can be credited with bringing the practice of mindfulness to the scientific and medical fields. His mindfulness-based stress reduction (MBSR) program, designed to increase individual well-being, manage stress, and help heal the unwell body, has paved the way for numerous clinical, psychological, and neuroscientific studies that have notably promoted mindfulness in the West. Kabat-Zinn has succeeded in his goal of creating a broadly accessible, practical "secular" version of the practice, thereby facilitating its widespread diffusion in Western societies, even in institutional settings such as hospitals, schools, and universities. Thanks to his pioneering work, the scientific study of mindfulness has seen extraordinary development in recent years. Various factors have contributed to that development, first and foremost the availability of progressively sophisticated research tools, with particular reference to neuroimaging techniques, which make it possible to study the activation and structure of the human brain during mindfulness and meditation practices. This was then bolstered by the involvement of leading research centers and institutes, in addition to the increasing number of articles on the topic that have been published in authoritative scientific journals. And of course, the mass media's growing interest in the topic, intrigued by the effect of mindfulness on people's mental and physical well-being and on the ability to overcome the mind-body dichotomy, which is so deeply rooted in the Western world, has played its part.

Today, we know with certainty that mindfulness can benefit people's lives. Different studies, including those in which our laboratory at Sapienza University of Rome has taken part, have shown that programs or interventions based on mindfulness can reduce stress and mental distress, helping people feel calmer and improving their concentration, resilience, and mental clarity. Training based on mindfulness has healthy effects on the brain, improving mental functioning and reducing the signs of cognitive aging. Our research also points to the possibility that training on meditation and mindfulness makes the use of the brain's energy more efficient, as it teaches people how to increase their focus on what is needed at a given time, without distraction.

Mindfulness and the meditative practices connected to it are thus an incredible resource at our disposal for the challenges of existence, both on an individual and societal level. And of course, ecological mindfulness can help change attitudes and behaviors in relation to the environment and the planet, particularly important at such a crucial moment in time, threatened as we are by environmental devastation and climate change on a global scale. Mindfulness may indeed help us be more resilient and to envision and do our part to create a sustainable future.

Antonino Raffone,

PhD, is an Associate Professor in the Psychology Department of Sapienza University of Rome, Director of the Mindfulness: Practice, Clinical Applications and Neuroscience master's program and of the ECONA Interuniversity Center at Sapienza University, and President of the Consciousness, Mindfulness, Compassion – CMC – International Association.

1

January

Sitting like a mountain
let your mind rise,
fly and soar.

– Sogyal Rinpoche

JANUARY

2

Be curious, not judgmental.

– Walt Whitman

3

January

Our opinions have no permanence;
like autumn and winter,
they gradually pass away.

– Chuang Tzu

4

January

Be happy for those who are happy,
have compassion towards the unhappy,
and maintain equanimity
towards the wicked.

– Patañjali

5

January

Get out of your head and get into
your heart. Think less, feel more.

– Osho

6

January

Like a clear, still pool without ripples,
mindfulness perfectly mirrors what's
occurring without distortion.

– Kristin Neff

7

January

That's life: starting over,
one breath at a time.

– Sharon Salzberg

8

January

True intelligence operates silently.
Stillness is where creativity and solutions to problems are found.

– Eckhart Tolle

9

January

A new day is here. Yesterday is a memory.
Tomorrow is unknown. Now is the knowing.

– Ajahn Sumedho

10

January

The only way to make sense out of change
is to plunge into it, move with it,
and join the dance.

– Alan W. Watts

11

January

Nothing ever goes away, until it has
taught us what we need to know.

– Pema Chödrön

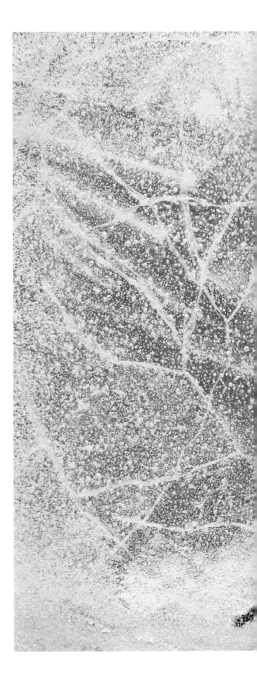

12
January

Don't curse the darkness,
light a candle.

– Confucius

13
January

If the only prayer you ever say
in your entire life is "thank you,"
it will be enough.

– Meister Eckhart

14
January

Breathing in, I calm body and mind.
Breathing out, I smile.
Dwelling in the present moment
I know this is the only moment.

– Thích Nhất Hạnh

15
January

I would like you to love
yourself, because unless
you love yourself you cannot
love anybody else.

– Osho

16

January

In spring, hundreds of flowers;
in autumn, a harvest moon;
In summer, a refreshing breeze;
in winter, snow will accompany you.
If useless things
do not hang in your mind,
any season is a good season for you.

– Wumen Huikai

17
January

Do not judge me by my success,
judge me by how many times I fell down
and got back up again.

– Nelson Mandela

18
January

If you wish to see the truth then
hold no opinion, for or against.

– Sēngcàn

19

January

You have only to rest in inaction
and things will transform themselves.

– Chuang Tzu

20

January

Before the rain stops, we hear a bird. Even under the heavy snow,
we see snowdrops and some new growth.

– Shunryū Suzuki

21
January

When we cannot find contentment
in ourselves, it is useless
to seek it elsewhere.

– François de La Rochefoucauld

22
January

To seek is to suffer.
To seek nothing is bliss.

– Bodhidharma

23

January

All men's miseries derive from not being able
to sit in a quiet room alone.

– Blaise Pascal

24

January

The simplest acts of kindness are by far more powerful
than a thousand heads bowing in prayer.

– Mahatma Gandhi

25

January

Drop the idea of becoming someone,
because you are already
a masterpiece.

– Osho

26

January

If your mind is empty,
it is always ready for anything;
it is open to everything.

– Shunryū Suzuki

27

January

Have good trust in yourself,
not in the one that you think you should be,
but in the one that you are.

– Taizan Maezumi

28

January

Rejoicing in ordinary things
is not sentimental or trite.
It actually takes guts.

– *Pema Chödrön*

29

January

There are only two ways to live
your life. One is as if nothing
is a miracle. The other is as if
everything is a miracle.

– *Albert Einstein*

30

January

Where are you running to?
Don't you know that Heaven is within you?

– Angelus Silesius

31

All know the way;
few actually walk it.

– Bodhidharma

1

February

You are your own teacher. Looking for teachers can't solve your own doubts. Investigate yourself to find the truth – inside, not outside. Knowing yourself is most important.

– Ajahn Chah

FEBRUARY

2

February

Awareness is like the sun. When it shines on things,
they are transformed.

– *Thích Nhất Hạnh*

3

February

Each moment is all we need,
nothing more.

– Mother Teresa

4

February

Kindness is like snow.
It beautifies everything it covers.

– Kahlil Gibran

5

February

As many times as I forget, catch myself
charging forward without even knowing
where I'm going, that many times
I can make the choice to stop, to breathe,
and be, and walk slowly into the mystery.

– Danna Faulds

6

February

We have only now, only this single eternal moment
opening and unfolding before us, day and night.

– Jack Kornfield

7
February

There's a voice that doesn't use words.
Listen!

– Jalāl al-Dīn Moḥammad Rūmī

8
February

Don't let life harden your heart.

– Pema Chödrön

9
February

Just as with her own life, a mother
shields from hurt her own son,
her only child, let all-embracing
thoughts for all beings be yours.

– The Buddha

10

February

Be at peace with everything, with the people you live
with, the places you go, the society you are part of.
But most of all, be at peace with yourself.

– Ajahn Sumedho

11

Looking at beauty in the world, is the first step
of purifying the mind.

– Amit Ray

12

Courage doesn't always roar. Sometimes courage is the quiet
voice at the end of the day saying: "I will try again tomorrow."

– Mary Anne Radmacher

13
February

We all have the ability to pay attention
to what we've lost, or to pay attention
to what we still have.

– Edith Eva Eger

14
February

Wise men don't judge:
they seek to understand.

– Wei Wu Wei

15

February

Think with your whole body.

– Taïsen Deshimaru

16

February

What you are now is the result of what you were. What you will be tomorrow will be the result of what you are now.

– Henepola Gunaratana

17

February

When you reach the top of the
mountain, keep climbing.

– Zen proverb

18

February

Think lightly of yourself
and deeply of the world.

– Miyamoto Musashi

19
February

A kind word can warm
three winter months.

– Chinese proverb

20
February

Let the breath lead the way.

– Sharon Salzberg

21

February

Every fact, every event of our day
is like a seed brought by the wind,
which lies in our heart; only with
silence and meditation every seed
will bring good fruits.

– Thomas Merton

22

February

I will be generous with my love today.
I will sprinkle compliments
and uplifting words everywhere I go.

– Steve Maraboli

23
February

Whatever life takes away from you,
let it go.

– Don Miguel Ruiz

24
February

Every experience is a lesson.
Every loss is a gain.

– Sathya Sai Baba

25
February

Perhaps the most "spiritual" thing
any of us can do is simply to look
through our own eyes,
see with eyes of wholeness,
and act with integrity and kindness.

– Jon Kabat-Zinn

26
February

My meditation is simple...
It is singing. It is dancing.
It is sitting silently.

– Osho

27
February

Waking up this morning, I smile.
Twenty-four brand new hours
are before me. I vow to live fully
in each moment and to look at all
beings with eyes of compassion.

– *Thích Nhất Hạnh*

28/29
February

The art of peaceful living comes down
to living compassionately and wisely.

– *Allan Lokos*

1

March

Happiness is your nature. It is not wrong to desire it.
What is wrong is seeking it outside when it is inside.

– Ramana Maharshi

MARCH

2

March

Always keep your mind as bright
and clear as the vast sky, the great
ocean, and the highest peak,
empty of all thoughts.

– Morihei Ueshiba

3

March

Every individual is an expression
of the whole realm of nature,
a unique action of the total universe.

– Alan W. Watts

4

March

Only those who know how to look at a tree,
at the stars, at the sparkling waters
of a torrent, in a state of utter abandon,
know what beauty is.
This state of real vision is Love.

– Jiddu Krishnamurti

5

March

The Way is not in the sky,
the Way is in the heart.

– The Buddha

6

March

I no longer agree to treat myself with disrespect. Every time a self-critical thought comes to mind, I will forgive the Judge and follow this comment with words of praise, self-acceptance, and love.

– Don Miguel Ruiz

7

March

Only a burning patience will lead to the attainment of a splendid happiness.

– Martha Medeiros

8
March

Mindfulness is a way of befriending
ourselves and our experience.

– Jon Kabat-Zinn

9
March

Just as a snake sheds its skin,
we must shed our past
over and over again.

– Jack Kornfield

10
March

Nothing is forever,
except change.

– The Buddha

11
March

Your heart is full of fertile seeds,
waiting to sprout.

– Morihei Ueshiba

12

March

Don't try to steer the river.

– Deepak Chopra

13

March

Rivers know this: there is no hurry.
We shall get there some day.

– A. A. Milne

14
March

In the midst of chaos,
there is also opportunity.

– *Sun Tzu*

15
March

You are not separate from the whole.
You are one with the sun, the earth,
the air. You don't have a life. You are life.

– Eckhart Tolle

16
March

Keep your hands open, and all the sands
of the desert can pass through them.
Close them, and all you can feel
is a bit of grit.

– Eihei Dōgen

17
March

The more you are motivated
by love, the more fearless
and free your action will be.

– Tenzin Gyatso, the 14th Dalai Lama

18
March

Let the wave of memory, the storm
of desire, the fire of emotion
pass through without affecting
your equanimity.

– Sathya Sai Baba

19
March

We are the same, you and I.
We are images of light.

– Don Miguel Ruiz

20
March

Those who are free of resentful
thoughts surely find peace.

– The Buddha

21
March

Looking for peace is like looking for
a turtle with a moustache: you won't be
able to find it. But when your heart is
ready, peace will come looking for you.

– Ajahn Chah

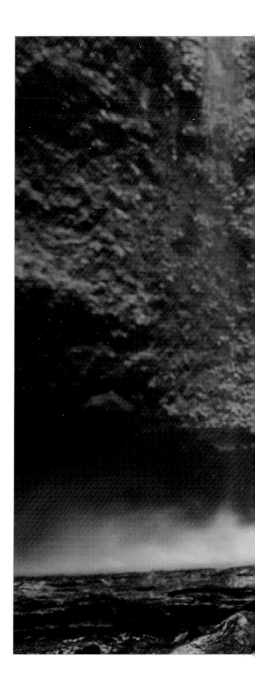

22
March

You are never alone. You are eternally
connected with everyone.

– Amit Ray

23
March

Use the power of your word
in the direction of truth and love.

– Don Miguel Ruiz

24

March

Let go, and the wave's crest will carry you to unknown shores,
beyond your wildest dreams or destinations.

– Danna Faulds

25

March

Life is a balance of holding on and letting go.

– Jalāl al-Dīn Moḥammad Rūmī

26
March

You are alive, so take your life
and enjoy it.

– Don Miguel Ruiz

27
March

Mastering others is strength;
mastering yourself is true power.

– Lao Tzu

28

March

The little things? The little moments?
They aren't little.

– Jon Kabat-Zinn

29

March

Just as parents care for their children,
you should bear in mind
the whole universe.

– Eihei Dōgen

30
March

Nature does not hurry,
yet everything is accomplished.

– Lao Tzu

31
March

There is no controlling life. Try corralling
a lightning bolt, containing a tornado.
Dam a stream and it will create a new
channel. Resist, and the tide will sweep
you off your feet. Allow, and grace
will carry you to higher ground.

– Danna Faulds

1

April

The art of living ... is neither careless drifting on the one hand
nor fearful clinging to the past on the other.
It consists in being sensitive to each moment,
in regarding it as utterly new and unique,
in having the mind open and wholly receptive.

– Alan W. Watts

APRIL

2
April

I wish you time – not time to spend
away. I wish that some of it may be left
for you as a time to marvel and to trust
instead of just looking at the time
on your watch.

– Elli Michler

3
April

Sitting quietly,
doing nothing,
spring comes,
and grass grows by itself.

– From the Zenrin-kushū

4

April

Nothing we see or hear is perfect.
But right there in the imperfection
is perfect reality.

– Shunryū Suzuki

5

April

Reality is created by the mind,
we can change our reality
by changing our mind.

– Plato

6

April

This very moment is the perfect
teacher, and, lucky for us,
it's with us wherever we are.

– Pema Chödrön

7

April

Direct your eye right inward, and you'll
find a thousand regions of your mind
yet undiscovered. Travel them and be
expert in home-cosmography.

– Henry David Thoreau

8

April

Feelings come and go
like clouds in a windy sky.
Conscious breathing is my anchor.

– Thích Nhất Hạnh

9

April

To live with an open heart
is to experience life full-strength.

– John Welwood

10
April

Follow the stream, have faith in its course. Just follow it. Never let it out of your sight. It will take you.

– Sheng-yen

11
April

Life begins where fear ends.

– Osho

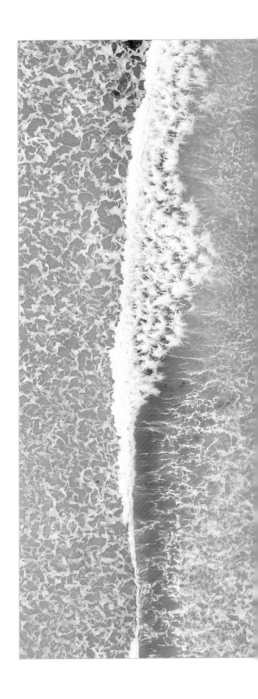

12

April

Whoever stills sustained thoughts
– as rain would, a cloud of dust –
through an awareness with thinking
stilled, attains right here
the state of peace.

– *Itivuttaka*

13

April

Health is the greatest gift,
contentment is the greatest wealth.

– The Buddha

14

April

Life is like riding a bicycle.
To keep your balance, you must keep moving.

– Albert Einstein

15
April

How sad that people ignore the near,
and search for truth afar:
like someone in the midst of water,
crying out in thirst.

– Hakuin Ekaku

16
April

Beauty is not who you are on the
outside, it is the wisdom and time
you gave away to save another
struggling soul like you.

– Shannon L. Alder

17
April

We have forgotten what rocks,
plants, and animals still know.
We have forgotten how to be – to be
still, to be ourselves, to be where life is:
Here and Now.

– Eckhart Tolle

18
April

When you realize nothing is lacking,
the whole world belongs to you.

– Lao Tzu

19
April

Set your heart on doing good.
Do it over and over again,
and you will be filled with joy.

– The Buddha

20
April

It is not joy that makes us grateful;
it is gratitude that makes us joyful.

– David Steindl-Rast

21

April

If you think you are too small to make a difference,
try sleeping with a mosquito.

– Tenzin Gyatso, the 14th Dalai Lama

22

April

I am larger, better than I thought, I did not know I held so much
goodness. All seems beautiful to me, I can repeat over to men and
women, You have done such good to me I would do the same to you.

– Walt Whitman

23
April

Don't waste your time chasing
butterflies. Mend your garden,
and the butterflies will come.

– Mario Quintana

24
April

My words are like seeds
and when they fall on fertile soil,
a reflection of those seeds
will grow into something greater.

– Steve Maraboli

25
April

The consequences of an evil mind will
follow you like the cart follows the ox
that pulls it. The consequences
of a purified mind will follow you
like your own shadow.

– Henepola Gunaratana

26
April

To be in harmony with the wholeness
of things is not to have anxiety
over imperfections.

– Eihei Dōgen

27
April

A flower does not think of competing
with the flower next to it.
It just blooms.

– Ogui Koshin

28
April

Everyone you meet is fighting a battle
you know nothing about.
Be kind. Always.

– Brad Meltzer

29

April

Seek out a tree
and let it teach you stillness.

– Eckhart Tolle

30

April

Patience is the key. Patience.
If you learn nothing else from
meditation, you will learn patience.

– Henepola Gunaratana

1

May

It was when I stopped searching for home within others
and lifted the foundations of home within myself
I found there were no roots more intimate
than those between a mind and body
that have decided to be whole.

– Rupi Kaur

2
May

Look at a tree, a flower, a plant.
Let your awareness rest upon it.
How still they are, how deeply rooted
in "just being." Allow nature
to teach you stillness.

– Eckhart Tolle

3
May

Knowing others is intelligence;
knowing yourself is true wisdom.

– Lao Tzu

4

May

You're under no obligation to be the same person
you were five minutes ago.

– Alan W. Watts

5

May

In this moment, there is plenty of time.
In this moment, you are precisely as you should be.

– Victoria Morgan

6

May

It's not the magnitude of the task that matters,
it's the magnitude of our courage.

– Matthieu Ricard

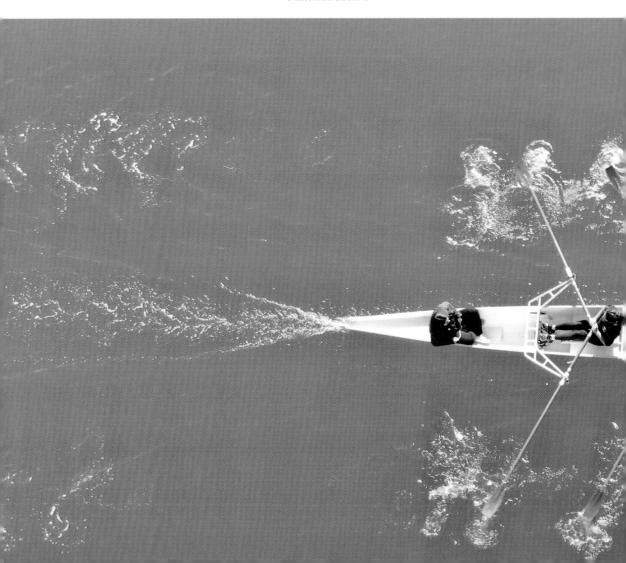

7

May

Stay in the centre, and you will be ready
to move in any direction.

– Alan W. Watts

8
May

Gratitude is the fairest blossom
which springs from the soul.

– Henry Ward Beecher

9
May

Don't insist on going
where you think you want to go.
Ask the way to the Spring. Your living
pieces will form a harmony.

– Jalāl al-Dīn Moḥammad Rūmī

10
May

A flower falls, even though
we love it; and a weed grows,
even though we do not love it.

– Eihei Dōgen

11
May

Happiness is when what you think,
what you say, and what you do
are in harmony.

– Mahatma Gandhi

12
May

The mind can go in a thousand
directions, but on this beautiful path
I walk in peace. With each step,
the wind blows. With each step,
a flower blooms.

– Thích Nhất Hạnh

13

May

Understanding is better than
mechanical practice. Meditation
is better than understanding. But best
of all is letting go of the anxiety
for the result, because this is
immediately followed by peace.

– Bhagavadgītā

14

May

Yesterday I was clever, so I wanted
to change the world. Today I am wise,
so I am changing myself.

– Jalāl al-Dīn Moḥammad Rūmī

15

May

If you love a flower, don't pick it up.
Because if you pick it up it dies
and it ceases to be what you love.
So if you love a flower, let it be.

– Osho

16

May

Generosity is the most natural outward
expression of an inner attitude
of compassion and loving-kindness.

– Tenzin Gyatso, the 14th Dalai Lama

17
May

A path is made
by walking on it.

– Chuang Tzu

18
May

We must anticipate with absolute
equanimity whatever may be coming
towards us, thinking only that
whatever it may be will be brought
to us by the wisdom-filled guidance
of the universe.

– Rudolf Steiner

19
May

Surrender to what is. Let go of what
was. Have faith in what will be.

– Sonia Ricotti

20

May

May our heart's garden of awakening
bloom with hundreds of flowers.

– Thích Nhất Hạnh

21
May

In the end, just three things matter:
how well we have lived, how well
we have loved, how well
we have learned to let go.

– Jack Kornfield

22
May

Love and compassion are necessities,
not luxuries. Without them,
humanity cannot survive.

– Tenzin Gyatso, the 14th Dalai Lama

23
May

Learning to let go should be learned
before learning to get.

– Ray Bradbury

24
May

Those who are possessed by nothing
possess everything.

– Morihei Ueshiba

25
May

Mindfulness means paying attention in a particular way:
on purpose, in the present moment, and non-judgmentally.

– Jon Kabat-Zinn

26

May

What a caterpillar calls the end of the world,
we call a butterfly.

– Eckhart Tolle

27
May

If with a pure mind a person speaks
or acts, happiness follows them like
a never-departing shadow.

– The Buddha

28
May

Do not look upon this world with fear
and loathing. Bravely face whatever
the gods offer.

– Morihei Ueshiba

29
May

Life is a balance
between rest and movement.

– Osho

30
May

Don't believe everything you think.
Thoughts are just that: thoughts.

– Allan Lokos

31

May

Be like a lotus. Let the beauty of your heart speak.
Be grateful to the mud, water, air and the light.

– Amit Ray

1

June

Sometimes fate is like a small sandstorm that keeps changing
directions. You change direction but the sandstorm chases you.
You turn again, but the storm adjusts. Over and over you play this out,
like some ominous dance with death just before dawn.
Why? Because this storm isn't something that blew in from far away,
something that has nothing to do with you.
This storm is you.

– Haruki Murakami

JUNE

2
June

Life is like an ever-shifting
kaleidoscope – a slight change,
and all patterns alter.

– Sharon Salzberg

3
June

Always keep your body filled with light
and heat. Fill yourself with the power
of wisdom and enlightenment.

– Morihei Ueshiba

4

June

One loses joy and happiness, in the attempt to possess them.

– Masanobu Fukuoka

5

June

There is nothing outside of yourself that can ever enable you
to get better, stronger, richer, quicker, or smarter.

– Miyamoto Musashi

6

June

Life isn't as serious as the mind makes it out to be.

– Eckhart Tolle

7

June

Love all. Serve all. Help ever. Hurt never.

– Sathya Sai Baba

8

June

I follow four dictates: face it, accept it,
deal with it, then let it go.

– Sheng-yen

9

June

Just as people have eyes to see light with and ears to hear sounds with,
so they have hearts for the appreciation of time. And all the time they
fail to appreciate is as wasted on them as the colours of the rainbow are
wasted on a blind person or the nightingale's song on a deaf one.

– Michael Ende

10
June

Muddy water is best cleared
by leaving it alone.

– Alan W. Watts

11
June

The place to improve the world
is first in one's own heart
and head and hands.

– Robert Maynard Pirsig

12
June

The difference between misery
and happiness depends on what
we do with our attention.

– Sharon Salzberg

13
June

Our life can be greatly transformed
by even a minimal change in how
we manage our thoughts and perceive
and interpret the world.

– Matthieu Ricard

14
June

Truth is not far away. It is nearer than near. There is no need to attain it, since not one of your steps leads away from it.

– *Eihei Dōgen*

15
June

If moment by moment you can keep your mind clear, then nothing will confuse you.

– *Sheng-yen*

16

June

He who is contented with contentment
shall be always content.

– Zen proverb

17

June

The first and the best victory
is to conquer self.

– Plato

18
June

Gratitude is the sign
of noble souls.

– Aesop

19
June

Whatever you think you are,
that's not what you are.

– Ajahn Sumedho

20
June

If your compassion does not include
yourself, it is incomplete.

– Jack Kornfield

21

June

A well-disciplined mind brings happiness.

– Henepola Gunaratana

22

June

Radiate boundless love towards the entire world.

– The Buddha

23

June

The first step toward personal freedom is awareness.

– Don Miguel Ruiz

24

June

The true purpose is to see things as they are,
to observe things as they are, and to let everything go as it goes.

– Shunryū Suzuki

25
June

I never think of the future –
it comes soon enough.

– Albert Einstein

26
June

We need much less
than we think we need.

– Maya Angelou

27
June

When it is obvious that the goals
cannot be reached, don't adjust the
goals, adjust the action steps.

– Confucius

28
June

Matters of great concern should
be treated lightly. Matters of small
concern should be treated seriously.

– Yamamoto Tsunetomo

29
June

These mountains that you are carrying,
you were only supposed to climb.

– Najwa Zebian

30
June

Keep your face always toward
the sunshine – and shadows
will fall behind you.

– Walt Whitman

1

July

In order to achieve silence, you would not chase the birds away because they make noise; in order to be still, you would not stop the movement of air or the rushing river, but accept them and you will yourself be aware of the silence.

– Chögyam Trungpa

JULY

2

July

Undying, untouched by fire or the
storms of life, there is a place inside
where stillness and abiding peace
reside. You can ride the breath
to go there.

– Danna Faulds

3

July

When we do not expect anything,
we can be ourselves.

– Shunryū Suzuki

4

July

Be generous with your energy.
Be generous with your smiles.

– Japanese proverb

5

July

Happiness is the absence
of the striving for happiness.

– Chuang Tzu

6

July

You can't stop the waves,
but you can learn to surf.

– Jon Kabat-Zinn

7

July

It is easy to believe we are each waves
and forget we are also the ocean.

– Jon J. Muth

8

July

Strengthening the mind is not done
by making it move around as is done
to strengthen the body, but by bringing
the mind to a halt, bringing it to rest.

– Ajahn Chah

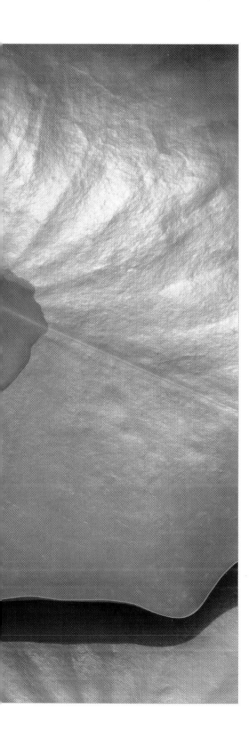

9
July

In the dew of little things the heart finds its morning and is refreshed.

– *Kahlil Gibran*

10
July

When you are born a lotus flower, be a beautiful lotus flower, don't try to be a magnolia flower. True happiness and true power lie in understanding yourself, accepting yourself, having confidence in yourself.

– *Thích Nhất Hạnh*

Joy is being willing for things to be as they are.

– Charlotte Joko Beck

12

July

Just one small positive thought in the morning
can change your whole day.

– Tenzin Gyatso, the 14th Dalai Lama

13
July

The only way to live is by accepting
each minute as an unrepeatable miracle.

– Tara Brach

14
July

We often take for granted the very
things that most deserve our gratitude.

– Cynthia Ozick

15
July

May you live every day of your life.

– Jonathan Swift

16
July

Sometimes the most important thing
in a whole day is the rest we take
between two deep breaths.

– Etty Hillesum

17

July

Resilience is accepting your new reality, even
if it's less good than the one you had before.
You can fight it, you can do nothing but
scream about what you've lost, or you can
accept that and try to put together
something that's good.

– Elizabeth Edwards

18

July

Awareness allows us to get
outside of our mind
and observe it in action.

– Dan Brulé

19
July

Move and the way will open.

– Zen proverb

20
July

Too lazy to be ambitious,
I let the world take care of itself.

– Ryōkan

21
July

Smile, breathe and go slowly.

– Thích Nhất Hạnh

22
July

Have the fearless attitude of a hero
and the loving heart of a child.

– Soyen Shaku

23
July

Forget the years, forget distinctions.
Leap into the boundless
and make it your home.

– Chuang Tzu

24
July

Sleep is the best meditation.

– Tenzin Gyatso, the 14th Dalai Lama

25
July

The present moment is filled
with joy and happiness.
If you are attentive, you will see it.

– Thích Nhất Hạnh

26
July

Be vigilant, always available, sharpen
your concentration like a sword.
Only then will you enter the Way.

– Taïsen Deshimaru

27
July

Failure is the key to success;
each mistake teaches us something.

– Morihei Ueshiba

28
July

Compassion and tolerance
are not a sign of weakness,
but a sign of strength.

– Tenzin Gyatso, the 14th Dalai Lama

29
July

What the superior man seeks
is in himself; what the small man
seeks is in others.

– Confucius

30

July

Life is a series of natural and spontaneous changes.
Don't resist them – that only creates sorrow.

– Lao Tzu

31

July

Even when the sky is heavily overcast, the sun hasn't disappeared. It's still there, on the other side of the clouds.

– Eckhart Tolle

1

August

If your mind is happy, then you're happy anywhere you go.
When wisdom awakens within you, you will see the Truth wherever
you look. Truth is all there is. It's like when you've learned how to
read – you can then read anywhere you go.

– Ajahn Chah

AUGUST

2
August

We shape clay into a pot,
but it is the emptiness inside
that holds whatever we want.

– Lao Tzu

3
August

The three elements of creativity are:
loving, knowing, and doing – or heart,
mind, and hands – or, as Zen Buddhist
teaching has it; great faith, great
question, and great courage.

– Eric Maisel

4
August

A man is great not because he hasn't failed; a man is great because failure hasn't stopped him.

– Confucius

5
August

When thoughts arise, then do all things arise. When thoughts vanish, then do all things vanish.

– Huang Po

6
August

Act without expectation.

– Lao Tzu

7

August

Attachment leads to suffering.

– The Buddha

8

August

Let go of the ways you thought life
would unfold, the holding of plans
or dreams or expectations – Let it all go.
Save your strength to swim with the tide.

– Danna Faulds

9

August

World peace must develop from inner peace.

– Tenzin Gyatso, the 14th Dalai Lama

10

August

A kind gesture can reach a wound that only compassion can heal.

– Steve Maraboli

11

August

The present moment is not an enemy
to be feared, but a dear friend
to be embraced.

– Jeff Foster

12

August

We must make good use of this life
for the time that we have left,
this brief flash of light, like the sun
appearing through the clouds.

– Kalu Rinpoche

13

August

Time does not change us.
It just unfolds us.

– Max Frisch

14

August

Now it is raining, but we don't know
what will happen in the next moment.
By the time we go out it may be a
beautiful day, or a stormy day.
Since we don't know, let's appreciate
the sound of the rain now.

– Shunryū Suzuki

15

August

Gratitude helps you to grow
and expand; gratitude brings joy
and laughter into your life and
into the lives of all those around you.

– Eileen Caddy

16
August

When you can't change the direction
of the wind – adjust your sails.

– H. Jackson Brown Jr.

17
August

There is no time to miss anyone
or anything, because you are alive.
Not enjoying what is happening right
now is living in the past and being
only half alive.

– Don Miguel Ruiz

18

August

If you haven't wept deeply,
you haven't begun to meditate.

– *Ajahn Chah*

19

August

Conquer anger with non-anger.
Conquer badness with goodness.
Conquer meanness with generosity.
Conquer dishonesty with truth.

– *The Buddha*

20

August

I would rather make mistakes in kindness
and compassion than work miracles in
unkindness and hardness.

– *Mother Teresa*

21

August

If you want others to be happy, practice compassion. If you want to be happy, practice compassion.

– Tenzin Gyatso, the 14th Dalai Lama

22

August

Do you have the patience to wait until your mud settles and the water is clear?

– Lao Tzu

23
August

While it may be difficult to change the world, it is always possible to change the way we look at it.

– Matthieu Ricard

24
August

When you really laugh, for those few moments you are in a deep meditative state. Thinking stops. It is impossible to laugh and think together.

– Osho

25

August

Let the flower of compassion blossom in the rich soil of loving kindness,
and water it with the good water of equanimity in the cool, refreshing shade of joy.

– Longchenpa

26

August

Do what you can, with what you have, where you are.

– Theodore Roosevelt

27
August

Men do not mirror themselves in running
water – they mirror themselves
in still water.

– Chuang Tzu

28
August

Your outer journey may contain a million
steps; your inner journey only has one:
the step you are taking right now.

– Eckhart Tolle

29
August

Be kind to yourself.
You may not be perfect, but you are
all you've got to work with.

– Henepola Gunaratana

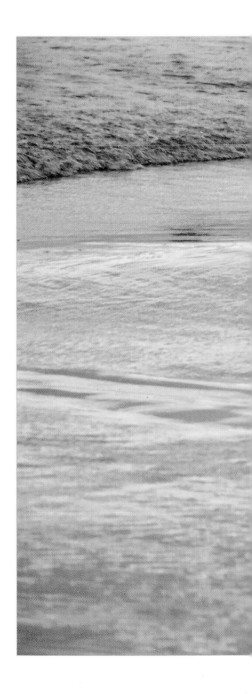

30
August

Don't seek, don't search,
don't ask, don't knock,
don't demand – relax.

– Osho

31
August

The perfect man uses his mind
like a mirror – going after nothing,
welcoming nothing, responding
but not storing.

– Chuang Tzu

1

September

If we have no peace, it is because we have forgotten
that we belong to each other.

– Mother Teresa

SEPTEMBER

2
September

Be still like a mountain
and flow like a great river.

– Lao Tzu

3
September

We each need to make our lion's roar
– to persevere with unshakable courage when
faced with all manner of doubts and sorrows
and fears – to declare our right to awaken.

– Jack Kornfield

4

September

When we give cheerfully and accept gratefully,
everyone is blessed.

– Maya Angelou

5

September

You have not lived today until you have done something for someone
who can never repay you.

– John Bunyan

6

September

Children are natural Zen masters; their world
is brand new in each and every moment.

– John Bradshaw

7

September

It is only through letting our heart break that we discover something unexpected: the heart cannot actually break, it can only break open.

– John Welwood

8

September

If you concentrate on finding whatever is good in every situation, you will discover that your life will suddenly be filled with gratitude, a feeling that nurtures the soul.

– Rabbi Harold Kushner

9

September

Every individual is a unique
manifestation of the Whole,
as every branch is a particular
outreaching of the tree.

– Alan W. Watts

10

September

The bamboo that bends is stronger
than the oak that resists.

– Japanese proverb

11

September

Hope is like a road in the country;
there was never a road, but when many
people walk on it, the road comes
into existence.

– Lin Yutang

12

September

The measure of intelligence
is the ability to change.

– Albert Einstein

13

September

Our mind can be our best friend
or our worst enemy.

– Matthieu Ricard

14

September

If you want to conquer the anxiety of life,
live in the moment, live in the breath.

– Amit Ray

15

September

When I'm riding my bicycle I feel like
a Buddhist who is happy just to enjoy
his mundane existence.

– Robin Williams

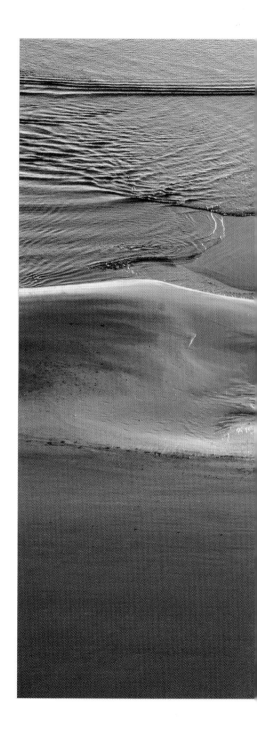

16
September

Everything – even mountains, rivers,
plants and trees – should be
your teacher.

– Morihei Ueshiba

17
September

Look at everything always as though
you were seeing it either for the first
or last time: thus is your time
on earth filled with glory.

– Betty Smith

18

September

Create each day anew by clothing
yourself with heaven and earth, bathing
yourself with wisdom and love,
and placing yourself in the heart
of Mother Nature.

– Morihei Ueshiba

19

September

Many people lose the small joys,
in the hope for the big happiness.

– Pearl S. Buck

20

September

Living is changing,
that's the lesson the seasons teach us.

– Paulo Coelho

21
September

Mindfulness is the aware, balanced acceptance
of the present experience.

– Sylvia Boorstein

22
September

I wish you the time for your doings
and thinking, not only for yourself,
but also to give away.
I wish you the time, not to hastle
and run, but time to learn
how to be happy.

– Elli Michler

23
September

Compassion is the basis
of morality.

– Arthur Schopenhauer

24
September

Everything is within.
Everything exists.

– Miyamoto Musashi

25
September

If you forget yourself,
you become the Universe.

– Hakuin Ekaku

26
September

Eternal life belongs to those
who live in the present.

– Ludwig Wittgenstein

27

September

No act of kindness, no matter how small,
is ever wasted.

– *Aesop*

28

September

The wise adapt themselves
to circumstances, as water molds
itself to the pitcher.

– Confucius

29

September

It does not matter how long you are
spending on the earth, how much
money you have gathered or how much
attention you have received.
It is the amount of positive vibration
you have radiated in life that matters.

– Amit Ray

30

September

Just as a prism refracts light differently
when you change its angle,
each experience of love illuminates love
in new ways, drawing from an infinite
palette of patterns and hues.

– Sharon Salzberg

1

Through our eyes, the universe is perceiving itself.
Through our ears, the universe is listening to its harmonies.
We are the witnesses through which the universe becomes conscious
of its glory, of its magnificence.

– Alan W. Watts

OCTOBER

2

October

The beauty and mystery of this world only emerge through affection,
attention, interest and compassion ... open your eyes wide and actually
see this world by attending to its colours, details and irony.

– Orhan Pamuk

3

October

Let reality be reality. Let things flow naturally forward
in whatever way they like.

– Lao Tzu

4

October

Balance is the perfect state of still
water. Let that be our model.
It remains quiet within and
is not disturbed on the surface.

– Confucius

5

October

On days when the sky is grey,
the sun has not disappeared forever.

– Arnaud Desjardins

6

October

Be kind whenever possible.
It is always possible.

– Tenzin Gyatso, the 14th Dalai Lama

7

October

Your spirit is the true shield.

– Morihei Ueshiba

8

October

Life is a dance.
Mindfulness is witnessing that dance.

– Amit Ray

9

October

Nothing is absolute. Everything changes,
everything moves, everything revolves,
everything flies and goes away.

– Frida Kahlo

10

October

I recognized happiness by the noise
it made when it left.

– Jacques Prévert

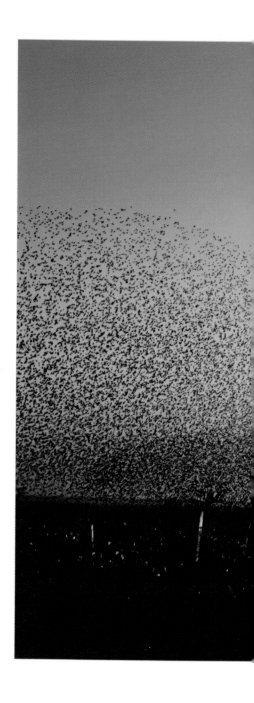

11

October

Gratitude is a powerful catalyst for happiness.
It's the spark that lights a fire of joy in your soul.

– Amy Collette

12

October

Thousands of candles can be lighted from a single candle,
and the life of the candle will not be shortened.
Happiness never decreases by being shared.

– The Buddha

13

October

Knowing yourself
is the beginning of all wisdom.

– Aristotle

14

October

Do nothing that is of no use.

– Miyamoto Musashi

15
October

The root of joy is gratefulness.

– David Steindl-Rast

16
October

In ordinary life, we hardly realize
that we receive a great deal more
than we give, and that it is only with
gratitude that life becomes rich.

– Dietrich Bonhoeffer

17
October

Wisdom says we are nothing.
Love says we are everything.
Between these two, our life flows.

– Jack Kornfield

18

October

All life is a manifestation of the spirit,
the manifestation of love.

– Morihei Ueshiba

19

October

Be happy in the moment, that's enough.

– Mother Teresa

20

October

To a mind that is still,
the entire universe surrenders.

– Chuang Tzu

21
October

Look well to this day
... today, if well-lived,
makes every yesterday
a memory of happiness,
and every tomorrow a vision of hope.
Look well, therefore, to this day.

– Kâlidâsa

22
October

Quiet the mind
and the soul will speak.

– Ma Jaya Sati Bhagavati

23

October

There is a crack in everything,
that's how the light gets in.

– Leonard Cohen

24

October

Smash your form and body,
spit out hearing and eyesight,
forget you are a thing among other
things, and you may join in great unity
with the deep and boundless.

– Chuang Tzu

25
October

When a person attains realization,
it is like the moon's reflection in water.
The moon never becomes wet; the water
is never disturbed. Although the moon
is a vast and great light, it is reflected
in a drop of water. The whole moon
and even the whole sky are reflected
in a drop of dew on a blade of grass.

– Eihei Dōgen

26
October

There is no small act of kindness.
Every compassionate act
makes large the world.

– Mary Anne Radmacher

27
October

Look past your thoughts, so you may
drink the pure nectar of This Moment.

– *Jalāl al-Dīn Moḥammad Rūmī*

28
October

This is the real secret of life –
to be completely engaged with what
you are doing in the here and now.
And instead of calling it work,
realize it is play.

– *Alan W. Watts*

29

October

The oak fought the wind
and was broken, the willow bent
when it must and survived.

– Robert Jordan

30

October

A single act of kindness throws out
roots in all directions, and the roots
spring up and make new trees.

– Amelia Earhart

31

October

To live fully is to be always
in no-man's land, to experience
each moment as completely new
and fresh. To live is to be willing
to die over and over again.

– Pema Chödrön

1

November

Do not permit the events of your daily
lives to bind you, but never withdraw
yourselves from them.

– Huang Po

NOVEMBER

When you have learned compassion for
yourself, compassion for others is automatic.

– *Henepola Gunaratana*

3

November

The secret of life is to fall seven times
and to get up eight times.

– Paulo Coelho

4

November

What wisdom can you find
that is greater than kindness?

– Jean-Jacques Rousseau

5
November

Be present in all things and thankful
for all things.

– Maya Angelou

6
November

I don't hold on to anything,
don't reject anything;
nowhere an obstacle or conflict.

– Layman P'ang

7

November

By the practice of meditation,
you will find that you are carrying
within your heart a portable paradise.

– Paramahansa Yogananda

8

November

A finger points at the moon,
but the moon is not at the tip
of the finger. Words point at the
truth, but the truth is not in words.

– Huinêng

9

November

What we call "I" is just
a swinging door which
moves when we inhale
and when we exhale.

– *Shunryū Suzuki*

10

November

To be wronged is nothing
unless you continue
to remember it.

– *Confucius*

11

November

Keep your heart clear and transparent,
and you will never be bound.
A single disturbed thought creates
ten thousand distractions.

– Ryōkan

12

November

Patience has all the time it needs.

– Allan Lokos

13

November

Let the beauty we love be what we do.

– Jalāl al-Dīn Moḥammad Rūmī

14

November

Your difficulties are not obstacles on the spiritual path,
they are the path.

– Ezra Bayda

15

November

Wherever you go, there you are.

– Jon Kabat-Zinn

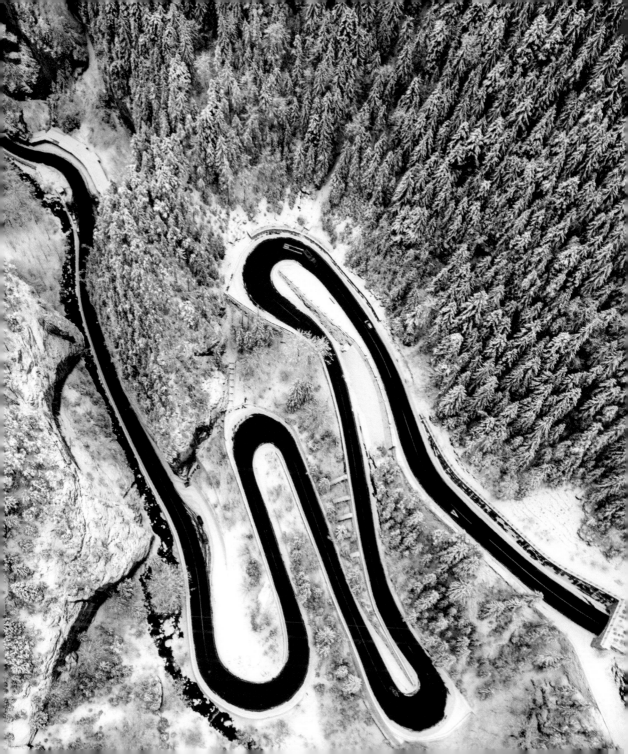

16
November

If you let go a little you will have a little
peace; if you let go a lot you will have
a lot of peace; if you let go completely,
you will have complete peace.

– Ajahn Chah

17
November

I love thinking of mindfulness simply
as the art of conscious living.

– Jon Kabat-Zinn

18

November

It is not the strongest of the species that survives,
nor the most intelligent that survives.
It is the one that is most adaptable to change.

– *Charles Darwin*

19

November

We can't choose to vanish the dark,
but we can choose to kindle the light.

– Edith Eva Eger

20

November

Gratitude is the most exquisite
form of courtesy.

– Jacques Maritain

21
November

If you cry because the sun has gone
out of your life, your tears will
prevent you from seeing the stars.

– Rabindranath Tagore

22
November

Accept everything,
just the way it is.

– Miyamoto Musashi

23

November

The best way to capture moments is to pay attention.

– Jon Kabat-Zinn

24

November

Gratitude, not understanding,
is the secret to joy and equanimity.

– Anne Lamott

25

November

There is a time to do away with old
clothes, the ones shaped to our body,
to forget the old path, always leading us
in the same direction. It's the crossing
point and if we don't dare do it,
we will remain forever
on the margins of ourselves.

– Fernando Pessoa

26
November

You are the sky.
Everything else
is just the weather.

– Pema Chödrön

27
November

Because you are alive,
everything is possible.

– Thích Nhất Hạnh

28

November

Patience is bitter, but its fruit is sweet.

– Jean-Jacques Rousseau

29
November

Peace of mind is that mental condition
in which you have accepted the worst.

– *Lin Yutang*

30
November

Speak with integrity.
Say only what you mean.

– *Don Miguel Ruiz*

1

December

It only takes a split second to smile and forget,
yet to someone that needed it, it can last a lifetime.

– *Steve Maraboli*

DECEMBER

2
December

Be master of mind rather
than mastered by mind.

– Zen proverb

3
December

Rest and be kind,
you don't have to prove anything.

– Jack Kerouac

4

December

The essence of bravery
is being without self-deception.

– Pema Chödrön

5

December

We have to make mistakes,
it's how we learn compassion for others.

– Curtis Sittenfeld

6

December

Real calmness should be found
in activity itself ... It is easy to have
calmness in inactivity, it is hard to have
calmness in activity, but calmness
in activity is true calmness.

– Shunryū Suzuki

7

December

If you shut the door to all errors,
truth will be shut out.

– Rabindranath Tagore

8

December

Do not seek the truth,
only cease to cherish your opinions.

– Sēngcàn

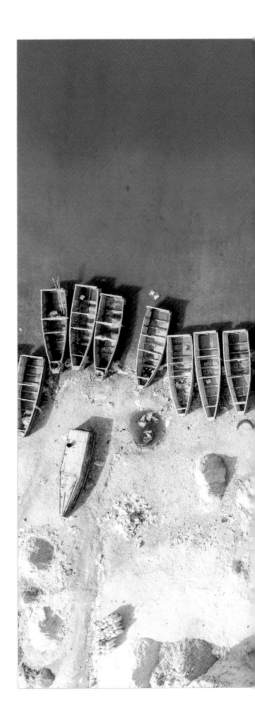

9

December

The heart is the only book worth reading.

– Ajahn Chah

10

December

When you do something, you should do it
with your whole body and mind.
You should do it completely, like a good
bonfire. You should burn yourself completely.

– Shunryū Suzuki

11

December

Fear is a natural reaction to moving
closer to the truth.

– Pema Chödrön

12

December

Difficulties and obstacles, if properly
understood and used, can turn out to
be an unexpected source of strength.

– Sogyal Rinpoche

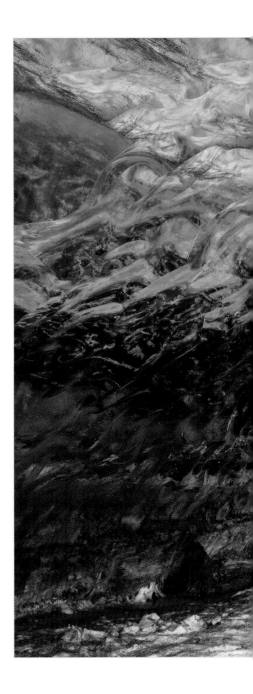

13

December

Let go of your worries
and be completely clear-hearted,
like the face of a mirror
that contains no images.
If you want a clear mirror,
behold yourself
and see the shameless truth,
which the mirror reflects.

– Jalāl al-Dīn Moḥammad Rūmī

14

December

The ability to observe without
evaluating is the highest
form of intelligence.

– Jiddu Krishnamurti

15

December

If you are depressed, you are living in
the past. If you are anxious, you are
living in the future. If you are at peace,
you are living in the present.

– Lao Tzu

16

December

Life is the dancer and you are the dance.

– Eckhart Tolle

17

December

Equanimity is a perfect, unshakable balance of mind.

– *Nyanaponika Thera*

18

December

Do not encumber your mind with
useless thoughts. What good is it
to brood over the past and fret about
the future? Dwell in the simplicity
of the present moment.

– Dilgo Khyentse Rinpoche

19

December

We cannot choose to have a life free
of hurt. But we can choose to be free,
to escape the past, no matter what
befalls us, and to embrace the possible.

– Edith Eva Eger

20

December

There are no strangers here;
only friends who haven't yet met.

– W. B. Yeats

21

December

To live – is that not enough?

– Daisetsu Teitarō Suzuki

22
December

What is stronger
than the human heart
which shatters over and over
and still lives.

– Rupi Kaur

23
December

We do not need guns and bombs
to bring peace, we need love
and compassion.

– Mother Teresa

24
December

Kindness is the language
which the deaf can hear
and the blind can see.

– Mark Twain

25

December

A certain darkness is needed
to see the stars.

– Osho

26

December

When you rise in the morning, give thanks
for the light, for your life, for your strength.
Give thanks for your food and for the joy of living.

– Tecumseh

27

December

When reading, only read.
When eating, only eat.
When thinking, only think.

– Seung Sahn

28

December

Let go or be dragged.

– Zen proverb

29
December

Constant kindness can accomplish much. As the sun makes ice melt, kindness causes misunderstanding, mistrust, and hostility to evaporate.

– Albert Schweitzer

30
December

Time is the coin of life. Only you can determine how it will be spent.

– Carl Sandburg

31

December

And now let us believe in a long year
that is given to us, new, untouched,
full of things that have never been.

– Rainer Maria Rilke

LIST OF AUTHORS

A

Aesop
(c. 620 BC – 564 BC)
Ancient Greek fabulist
and storyteller.
6/18 – 9/27

Ajahn Chah
(1918 – 1992)
Thai abbot and Buddhist monk.
2/1 – 3/21 – 7/8 – 8/1
8/18 – 11/16 – 12/9

Ajahn Sumedho
(1934 – living)
Buddhist monk and American
author.
1/9 – 2/10 – 6/19

Alder, Shannon L.
(living)
American writer.
4/16

Angelou, Maya
(1928 – 2014)
American poet, memoirist,
and civil rights activist.
6/26 – 9/4 – 11/5

Aristotle
(384 BC – 322 BC)
Ancient Greek philosopher
and scientist.
10/13

B

Bayda, Ezra
(1944 – living)
American writer and Zen teacher.
11/14

Beck, Charlotte Joko
(1917 – 2011)
American writer and Zen
teacher.
7/11

Beecher, Henry Ward
(1813 – 1887)
American clergyman, famous
for his antislavery speeches
and his advocacy of women's
suffrage.
5/8

Bhagavadgītā
(c. 2nd century BC)
Sacred Hindu scripture, commonly
dated to the second century BC.
5/13

Bodhidharma
(c. 483 – 540)
Persian Buddhist monk.
First patriarch of Zen Buddhism
in China.
1/22 – 1/31

Bonhoeffer, Dietrich
(1906 – 1945)
Lutheran pastor, theologian, poet,
and anti-Nazi dissident.
10/16

Boorstein, Sylvia
(1936 – living)
American author, psychotherapist,
and Buddhist teacher.
9/21

Brach, Tara
(1953 – living)
American psychologist, author,
and proponent of Buddhist
meditation.
7/13

Bradbury, Ray
(1920 – 2012)
American author. He worked in a
variety of genres including fantasy
and science fiction.
5/23

Bradshaw, John
(1933 – 2016)
American author.
9/6

Brown, H. Jackson, Jr.
(1940 – living)
American author.
8/16

Brulé, Dan
(living)
Modern-day teacher, healer, and a
world-renown pioneer in the field
of Breathwork. He is one of the
creators of Breath Therapy.
7/18

Buck, Pearl S.
(1892 – 1973)
American writer and novelist. In
1938, she was awarded the Nobel
Prize in Literature.
9/19

Buddha, The
(566 BC – 486 BC)
Monk, philosopher, sage, teacher,
and religious leader on whose
teachings Buddhism was founded.
2/9 – 3/5 – 3/10 – 3/20 – 4/13 – 4/19
5/27 – 6/22 – 8/7 – 8/19 – 10/12

Bunyan, John
(1628 – 1688)
English writer, theologian, and
preacher.
9/5

C

Caddy, Eileen
(1917 – 2006)
Spiritual teacher and new age
author, best known as one of
the founders of the Findhorn
Foundation community.
8/15

Chinese proverb
2/19

Chopra, Deepak
(1946 – living)
Indian-American author
and alternative-medicine
advocate.
3/12

Chuang Tzu
(c. 369 BC – c. 286 BC)
Influential Chinese philosopher.
He is credited with writing a work
known by his name (Zhuāngzǐ),
which is one of the foundational
texts of Taoism.
1/3 – 1/19 – 5/17 – 7/5 – 7/23 – 8/27
8/31 – 10/20 – 10/24

Coelho, Paulo
(1947 – living)
Brazilian lyricist and novelist.
9/20 – 11/3

Cohen, Leonard
(1934 – 2016)
Canadian singer-songwriter,
poet, and novelist.
10/23

Collette, Amy
(living)
American author.
10/11

Confucius
(551 BC – 479 BC)
Chinese philosopher.
1/12 – 6/27 – 7/29 – 8/4 – 9/28
10/4 – 11/10

D

Darwin, Charles
(1809 – 1882)
English naturalist, geologist, and
biologist, best known for his
contributions to the science of
evolution.
11/18

Desjardins, Arnaud
(1925 – 2011)
French author.
10/5

Dilgo Khyentse Rinpoche
(1910 – 1991)
Buddhist meditation master,
scholar, philosopher, and
poet.
12/18

E

Earhart, Amelia
(1897 – 1937)
American aviation pioneer.
10/30

Edwards, Elizabeth
(1949 – 2010)
American attorney, author, and
health care activist.
7/17

Eger, Edith Eva
(1927 – living)
American psychologist, writer,
and Holocaust survivor.
2/13 – 11/19 – 12/19

Eihei Dōgen
(1200 – 1253)
Japanese Buddhist priest, writer, poet, philosopher, and founder of the Sōtō school of Zen in Japan.
3/16 – 3/29 – 4/26 – 5/10 – 6/14 – 10/25

Einstein, Albert
(1879 – 1955)
German-born physicist who developed the special and general theories of relativity and won the Nobel Prize in Physics in 1921.
1/29 – 4/14 – 6/25 – 9/12

Ende, Michael
(1929 – 1995)
German writer.
6/9

F

Faulds, Danna
(living)
American yoga teacher, writer, and poet.
2/5 – 3/24 – 3/31 – 7/2 – 8/8

Foster, Jeff
(1980 – living)
English author.
8/11

Frisch, Max
(1911 – 1991)
German-speaking Swiss architect and author.
8/13

Fukuoka, Masanobu
(1913 – 2008)
Japanese farmer and philosopher celebrated for his natural farming and re-vegetation of desertified lands.
6/4

G

Gandhi, Mahatma
(1869 – 1948)
Indian lawyer, teacher, philosopher, and political ethicist.
1/24 – 5/11

Gibran, Kahlil
(1883 – 1931)
Lebanese-American writer, poet, and painter.
2/4 – 7/9

H

Hakuin Ekaku
(1686 – 1769)

Buddhist monk and Japanese Zen master.
4/15 – 9/25

Henepola Gunaratana
(1927 – living)
Sri Lankan Buddhist monk and author.
2/16 – 4/25 – 4/30 – 6/21 – 8/29 – 11/2

Hillesum, Etty
(1914 – 1943)
Writer, religious thinker, and victim of Nazi genocide.
7/16

Huang Po
(9th century AD)
Buddhist monk and Chinese Zen master.
8/5 – 11/1

Huìnéng
(638 – 713)
Chinese Buddhist monk.
11/8

I

Itivuttaka
Buddhist scripture, part of the Pāli Canon of Theravāda Buddhism.
4/12

J

Japanese proverb
7/4 – 9/10

Jiddu, Krishnamurti
(1895 – 1986)
Indian speaker and writer.
3/4 – 12/14

Jordan, Robert
(1948 – 2007)
American author of epic fantasy.
10/29

K

Kabat-Zinn, Jon
(1944 – living)
American professor emeritus of medicine and the creator of the Stress Reduction Clinic and the Center for Mindfulness in Medicine, Health Care, and Society at the University of Massachusetts Medical School.
2/25 – 3/8 – 3/28 – 5/25 – 7/6 – 11/15 11/17 – 11/23

Kahlo, Frida
(1907 – 1954)
Mexican painter.
10/9

Kālidāsa
(4th – 5th cent. AD)
Ancient India's greatest playwright and dramatist.
10/21

Kalu Rinpoche
(1905 – 1989)
Tibetan Buddhist lama, meditation master, scholar, and teacher.
8/12

Kaur, Rupi
(1992 – living)
Indian-born Canadian poet, illustrator, and author.
5/1 – 12/22

Kerouac, Jack
(1922 – 1969)
American novelist. He was a pioneer of the Beat Generation.
12/3

Kornfield, Jack
(1945 – living)
Author, Buddhist practitioner, and one of the key teachers to introduce Buddhist mindfulness practice to the West.
2/6 – 3/9 – 5/21 – 6/20 – 9/3 – 10/17

Kushner, Harold
(1935 – living)
American rabbi and popular author.
9/8

L

Lamott, Anne
(1954 – living)
American writer.
11/24

Lao Tzu
(6th century BC)
Chinese philosopher and writer.
3/27 – 3/30 – 4/18 – 5/3 – 7/30 – 8/2 8/6 – 8/22 – 9/2 – 10/3 – 12/15

La Rochefoucauld, François de
(1613 – 1680)
French moralist and author of maxims and memoirs.
1/21

Lin Yutang
(1895 – 1976)
Chinese novelist, essayist, and translator.
9/11 – 11/29

Lokos, Allan
(about 1940 – living)
Author and founder and guiding teacher of the Community Meditation Center located in New York City.
2/28–29 – 5/30 – 11/12

Longchenpa
(1308 – 1364)
Great luminary of Tibetan Buddhism.
8/25

M

Maisel, Eric
(1947 – living)
American psychotherapist, teacher, and author.
8/3

Ma Jaya Sati Bhagavati
(1940 – 2012)
American spiritual teacher.
10/22

Mother Teresa
(1910 – 1997)
Albanian-Indian Roman Catholic nun and missionary. She was awarded the 1979 Nobel Peace Prize.
2/3 – 8/20 – 9/1 – 10/19 – 12/23

Mandela, Nelson
(1918 – 2013)
Anti-apartheid revolutionary, political leader, and philanthropist who served as president of South Africa from 1994 to 1999.
1/17

Maraboli, Steve
(1975 – living)
American motivational speaker and author.
2/22 – 4/24 – 8/10 – 12/1

Maritain, Jacques
(1882 – 1973)
French philosopher and author.
11/20

Medeiros, Martha
(1961 – living)
Brazilian writer and journalist.
3/7

Meister Eckhart
(c. 1260 – c. 1328)
German theologian, philosopher, and mystic.
1/13

Meltzer, Brad
(1970 – living)
American novelist and comic book author.
4/28

Merton, Thomas
(1915 – 1968)
American Trappist monk and writer.
2/21

Michler, Elli
(1923 – 2014)
German poet.
4/2 – 9/22

Milne, A. A.
(1882 – 1956)
English author, best known for his books about the teddy bear Winnie-the-Pooh.
3/13

Miyamoto Musashi
(1584 – 1645)
Japanese swordsman and writer.
2/18 – 6/5 – 9/24 – 10/14 – 11/22

Morgan, Victoria
(living)
American writer.
5/5

Morihei Ueshiba
(1883 – 1969)
Japanese martial artist and founder of the martial art of Aikido.
3/2 – 3/11 – 5/24 – 5/28 – 6/3 – 7/27
9/16 – 9/18 – 10/7 – 10/18

Murakami, Haruki
(1949 – living)
Japanese writer.
6/1

Muth, Jon J.
(1960 – living)
American comic book artist and children's book illustrator.
7/7

N

Neff, Kristin
(1966 – living)

Associate professor in the University of Texas at Austin's Department of Educational Psychology. She created the Self-compassion Scales.
1/6

Nyanaponika Thera
(1901 – 1994)
Buddhist monk and one of the greatest authorities on Theravāda Buddhism.
12/17

O

Ogui, Koshin
(1940 – living)
Priest of the Jodo Shin Shu.
4/27

Osho
(1931 – 1990)
Indian mystic, guru, and spiritual teacher.
1/5 – 1/15 – 1/25 – 2/26 – 4/11 – 5/15
5/29 – 8/24 – 8/30 – 12/25

Ozick, Cynthia
(1928 – living)
American writer.
7/14

P

Pamuk, Orhan
(1952 – living)
Turkish novelist and essayist.
10/2

P'ang, Layman
(740 – 808)
Lay Buddhist in the Chinese Zen tradition.
11/6

Paramahansa Yogananda
(1893 – 1952)
Indian monk, yogi, and guru.
11/7

Pascal, Blaise
(1623 – 1662)
French mathematician, physicist, philosopher, and theologian.
1/23

Patañjali
(c. 200 BC – c. 150 BC)
Indian sage and author of the Yoga Sūtras, one of the foundational texts of classical Yoga philosophy.
1/4

Pema Chödrön
(1936 – living)
American Buddhist teacher, author, and nun.
1/11 – 1/28 – 2/8 – 4/6 – 10/31
11/26 – 12/4 – 12/11

Pessoa, Fernando
(1888 – 1935)
Portuguese poet and writer.
11/25

Pirsig, Robert Maynard
(1928 – 2017)
American writer and philosopher. He was the author of the philosophical novel *Zen and the Art of Motorcycle Maintenance*.
6/11

Plato
(428/427 BC – 348/347 BC)
Ancient Greek philosopher and writer.
4/5 – 6/17

Prévert, Jacques
(1900 – 1977)
French poet and screenwriter.
10/10

Q

Quintana, Mario
(1906 – 1994)
Brazilian poet and writer.
4/23

R

Rabindranath Tagore
(1861 – 1941)
Indian poet, writer, playwright, and philosopher from Bengal.
11/21 – 12/7

Radmacher, Mary Anne
(1957 – living)
American writer and artist.
2/12 – 10/26

Ray, Amit
(1960 – living)
Indian author and spiritual master.
2/11 – 3/22 – 5/31 – 9/14 – 9/29 –
10/8

Ramana Maharshi
(1879 – 1950)
Indian sage, he was one of the most significant spiritual teachers

to emerge from India during the first half of the 20th century.
3/1

Ricard, Matthieu
(1946 – living)
French writer and Buddhist monk.
5/6 – 6/13 – 8/23 – 9/13

Ricotti, Sonia
(1965 – living)
Writer and leading expert in personal transformation.
5/19

Rilke, Rainer Maria
(1875 – 1926)
Bohemian-Austrian poet and novelist.
12/31

Roosevelt, Theodore
(1858 – 1919)
American statesman who served as the 26th president of the United States. He was awarded the Nobel Peace Prize.
8/26

Rousseau, Jean-Jacques
(1712 – 1778)
Genevan philosopher, writer, and composer.
11/4 – 11/28

Ruiz, Don Miguel
(1952 – living)
Mexican author.
2/23 – 3/6 – 3/19 – 3/23 – 3/26
6/23 – 8/17 – 11/30

Rūmī, Jalāl al-Dīn Moḥammad
(1207 – 1273)
Persian poet, Islamic scholar, theologian, and Sufi mystic.
2/7 – 3/25 – 5/9 – 5/14 – 10/27 –11/13
12/13

Ryōkan
(1758 – 1831)
Japanese Buddhist monk and poet.
7/20 – 11/11

S

Salzberg, Sharon
(1952 – living)
American author and teacher of Buddhist meditation practices.
1/7 – 2/20 – 6/2 – 6/12 – 9/30

Sandburg, Carl
(1878 – 1967)
American poet.
12/30

Sathya Sai Baba
(1926 – 2011)
Indian spiritual master.
2/24 – 3/18 – 6/7

Schopenhauer, Arthur
(1788 – 1860)
German author and
philosopher.
9/23

Schweitzer, Albert
(1875 – 1965)
Alsatian theologian, organist,
writer, humanitarian, philosopher,
and physician.
12/29

Sēngcàn
(529 – 606)
Chinese Buddhist monk.
1/18 – 12/8

Seung Sahn
(1927 – 2004)
Korean Zen master.
12/27

Sheng-yen
(1931 – 2009)
Chinese Buddhist monk, religious
scholar, and teacher of Zen
Buddhism.
4/10 – 6/8 – 6/15

Shunryū Suzuki
(1904 – 1971)
Sōtō Zen monk and teacher
who helped popularize
Zen Buddhism in the
United States.
1/20 – 1/26 – 4/4 – 6/24 – 7/3 – 8/14
11/9 – 12/6 –12/10

Silesius, Angelus
(1624 – 1677)
German poet and mystic.
1/30

Sittenfeld, Curtis
(1975 – living)
American writer.
12/5

Smith, Betty
(1896 – 1972)
American writer.
9/17

Sogyal Rinpoche
(1947 – 2019)
World-renowned Buddhist
teacher and author from Tibet.
1/1 – 12/12

Soyen Shaku
(1860 – 1919)
The first Zen Buddhist master to
teach in the United States.
7/22

Steindl-Rast, David
(1926 – living)
American Catholic Benedictine
monk, author, and lecturer.
4/20 – 10/15

Steiner, Rudolf
(1861 – 1925)
Austrian philosopher and educator.
5/18

Sun Tzu
(544 BC – 496 BC)
Chinese general and philosopher.
3/14

Suzuki, Daisetsu Teitarō
(1870 – 1966)
Japanese author of books and
essays on Buddhism and Zen.
12/21

Swift, Jonathan
(1667 – 1745)
Irish poet and writer.
7/15

T

Taïsen Deshimaru
(1914 – 1982)
Zen Buddhist monk and teacher.
2/15 – 7/26

Taizan Maezumi
(1931 – 1995)
Japanese Zen Buddhist teacher.
1/27

Tecumseh
(1768 – 1813)
A Shawnee leader who became
the primary leader of a large

Native American confederacy in
the early 19th century.
12/26

**Tenzin Gyatso, the 14th Dalai
Lama**
(1935 – living)
Tibetan Buddhist monk, the
current Dalai Lama, the highest
spiritual leader of Tibet.
3/17 – 4/21 – 5/16 – 5/22 – 7/12
7/24 – 7/28 – 8/9 – 8/21 – 10/6

Thich Nhất Hạnh
(1926 – living)
Vietnamese Buddhist monk, poet,
and peace activist.
1/14 – 2/2 – 2/27 – 4/8 – 5/12 – 5/20
7/10 – 7/21 – 7/25 – 11/27

Thoreau, Henry David
(1817 – 1862)
American philosopher, writer,
and poet.
4/7

Tolle, Eckhart
(1948 – living)
Spiritual teacher and best-selling
author.
1/8 – 3/15 – 4/17 – 4/29 – 5/2 – 5/26
6/6 – 7/31 – 8/28 – 12/16

Trungpa, Chögyam
(1939 – 1987)
Author, philosopher, and Tibetan
Buddhist meditation master.
7/1

Twain, Mark
(1835 – 1910)
American writer.
12/24

W

Watts, Alan W.
(1915 – 1973)
English author and
philosopher.
1/10 – 3/3 – 4/1 – 5/4 – 5/7 – 6/10
9/9 – 10/1 – 10/28

Wei Wu Wei
(1895 – 1986)
Pen name of Terence James
Stannus Gray, an English theater
producer.
2/14

Welwood, John
(1943 – 2019)
American clinical psychologist,
psychotherapist, teacher, and author.
4/9 – 9/7

Whitman, Walt
(1819 – 1892)
American poet, essayist, and
journalist. Whitman is among
the most influential poets in the
American canon, often called the
father of free verse.
1/2 – 4/22 – 6/30

Williams, Robin
(1951 – 2014)
American actor and comedian.
9/15

Wittgenstein, Ludwig
(1889 – 1951)
Austrian-British philosopher
who worked primarily in logic,
the philosophy of mathematics,
the philosophy of mind, and the
philosophy of language.
9/26

Wumen Huikai
(1183 – 1260)
Chinese Zen master.
1/16

Y

Yamamoto Tsunetomo
(1659 – 1719)
Japanese samurai and philosopher.
6/28

Yeats, W. B.
(1865 – 1939)
Irish poet, dramatist, and prose
writer.
12/20

Z

Zebian, Najwa
(1990 – living)
Lebanese-Canadian activist,
author, and poet.
6/29

Zen proverb
2/17 – 6/16 – 7/19 – 12/2 – 12/28

Zenrin-kushū
Collection of Zen writings
(15th century)
4/3

PHOTO CREDITS

Introduction
Antonino Raffone

Edited
Studio Editoriale Brillante s.r.l.

Project Editor
Valeria Manferto De Fabianis

Graphic Designer
Paola Piacco

Editorial coordination
Giorgio Ferrero

WS White Star Publishers® is a registered trademark property of White Star s.r.l.

© 2021 White Star s.r.l.
Piazzale Luigi Cadorna, 6
20123 Milan, Italy
www.whitestar.it

ISBN 978-88-544-1791-5
1 2 3 4 5 6   25 24 23 22 21

Printed in Turkey